QUEEN
A Magic Tour

GW00499600

design
Richard Gray

photography
Denis O'Regan

additional photographs
Neal Preston
Torleif Svensson
Richard Young
Richard Gray

text
Peter Hillmore

SIDGWICK & JACKSON
LONDON

IMP
International Music Publications Limited

First published in Great Britain in
1987 by Sidgwick & Jackson Limited
in association with
International Music Publications Limited

© 1987 Queen Productions Limited

All Rights Reserved. No part of this publication
may be reproduced, stored in a retrieval system,
or transmitted in any form or by any means, electronic,
mechanical, photocopying, recording or otherwise,
without the prior permission of the Copyright owner

ISBN 0-283-99488-6

Printed in Great Britain by Panda Press

Sidgwick & Jackson Limited
1 Tavistock Chambers
Bloomsbury Way
London WC1A 2SC

International Music Publications Limited
Woodford Trading Estate
Southend Road
Woodford Green
Essex IG8 8HN

The strangest concert, and the one with its own kind of magic, had to be the one in Budapest. On the face of it, it was no different from any of the others all over Europe; the huge stage was in position in the city's largest stadium, its vast array of lights making it seem like a fairy grotto, the smoke pouring from the wings turning it into a witches' cauldron, awaiting the arrival of the magicians.

The courtiers to Queen had arrived some days earlier, driving across Europe in 15 huge lorries transporting the huge 180 foot long stage. It had taken the road crew of 60 something like two days to construct, untangling eight miles of cable, setting up five generators and erecting two giant 60 foot towers, festooned with searchlights.

Tickets had sold out weeks before and there were forlorn groups of unlucky people hanging around outside. The crowd filled every seat and every square inch of grass in the stadium. They listened to the supporting groups one of whom performed a bizarre 'Honky Tonk Woman' with a backing chorus of 20 women in peasant costume, twirling handkerchiefs, giving you some idea of what the Hungarians normally get. Don't even try to imagine what it sounded like. They waited patiently and excitedly. Darkness fell, the noise of the crowd rose, the stage lights flashed even more brightly and the smoke billowed even more violently – and out of the mist, Queen came on stage. Freddie Mercury began to flash like the lights and chase the smoke around the stage. Roger Taylor crouched behind his drums pounding out the rhythm, seemingly intent on smashing them to oblivion; John Deacon's face was tight with concentration as he played his bass, and Brian May fought a musical duel with Freddie Mercury. "One Vision" was an apt title for the opening number.

It was a familiar and exhilarating sight to every Queen fan. But it was different for the audience in Budapest. It wasn't only the first time they had ever seen Queen, it was also the first time an open air rock concert had ever taken place in the country, or behind the Iron Curtain, for that matter. While Queen fans all over Europe knew how to react, what to expect, were familiar with the theatricals and the stage show, the Hungarians were totally unprepared. From the moment the band arrived in Budapest, travelling from Vienna down the Danube in the hydrofoil last used by Mr Gorbachev, they were like people from another world. On stage, they looked like creatures from a different planet. The British Embassy was stunned as well, throwing a party for them, where sophisticated diplomats jostled each other to get autographs.

When Queen appeared on stage at the People's Stadium, you could almost hear the sound of 80,000 brains boggling. While their eyes became accustomed to the kaleidoscope of lights, their ears tuned into the music and their brains came to terms with the unusual sight of Freddie Mercury, there was a moment of stunned and bewildered silence as the fans – some of whom had even come from as far away as Russia – tried to decide on the correct way to react to what they saw in front of them. For days earlier, the local newspapers had been printing guides to rock concert etiquette, and cautioning calm. Even Queen themselves, used to playing before audiences who know their music and are accustomed to their stage behaviour had been more than usually apprehensive, not knowing what would happen. The authorities had pompously, and nervously announced before the concert that they were going to be "lenient towards the behaviour of young people" at the concert, but the presence of a few armed soldiers indicated that they, too, didn't know how people would react (Brian May was to say afterwards that "it was the band's most challenging and exhilarating gig").

The Hungarians had assembled 17 cameras to film this strange phenomenon that had arrived from the west, even if it never happened again, there would be proof behind the Iron Curtain that Freddie Mercury actually existed and the concert had really taken place, just in case children were to doubt it all in years to come.

You have to agree that the strange sight of Freddie Mercury in perpetual motion, the gigantic noise of Queen in full flight, and the sheer spectacle of the stage show is a hell of an introduction to rock concerts (and western decadence, liable to inflame the passions); but it was only a moment of indecision and bewilderment. Before long, the audience were behaving like audiences all over Europe. The familiar two way drip feed of adrenalin had been set up, the band fuelling the crowd with energy, and this energy from the crowd travelling back goading the band into even greater activity. The power of rock and roll and the universal love of theatricals exerted themselves, and soon everybody was singing along with the band, not frowning but waving. The words "Radio-Ga-Ga" seem to translate quite easily into every known language, and 80,000 pairs of hands miraculously knew how to perform the traditional synchronised handclap that goes with the song. Freddie made his final entrance, stripped to the waist, wearing the jewelled crown of a monarch, his baton doubling as a regal sceptre. He was swathed in a Union Jack, with the Hungarian national flag embroidered on the back. The people of Budapest hadn't seen anything like it since Peter the Great, but the crescendo of noise from the band and crowd alike was as exhilarating and as familiar as it had been all over the rest of Europe.

After 15 years, finding enough people who have never seen Queen live to fill a stadium in 1986 was quite an achievement. With over 80 million records sold all over the world, they're not exactly unknowns. There aren't many bands who could fill Wembley stadium for one night, let alone two. There aren't many bands who could draw 120,000 fans to Knebworth in one of the biggest concerts in pop history, the largest single paying audience for a UK rock concert in over ten years. And the historic event was also marked by probably the biggest traffic jam in British history. As the fans converged on the historic 15th century house and huge grounds of Knebworth, the authorities, in their wisdom, chose Saturday, August 9, to close most of the A1 close to the site. People still managed to reach Knebworth for a day of rock (Status Quo flew in from a concert the day before in Scandinavia, as soon as their set was over they ran for helicopters which would take them to another, late night gig in Switzerland a few hours

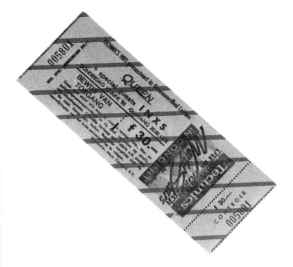

later). The road crew had driven non-stop from the previous concert Marbella, to erect the stage. Everybody made it, just (during the concert, a woman went into labour as a new Queen fan arrived, later than most).

Darkness had fallen. The security men were performing the traditional pagan rite of hurling buckets of water over the long suffering fans who had positioned themselves at the front of the stage many hours earlier. A few impatient fans were already holding lighters and matches aloft in the ceremony that is supposed to end concerts, rather than occur mid way through. Backstage, Freddie Mercury was finishing his traditional 30 minutes of physical exercises and was running his voice up and down through the scales. Queen had been on the road since the beginning of June, and had played to astonishing numbers of people somewhere, amid the crowd at Knebworth was the millionth member of the European audience (perhaps it was the baby).

Then it was show time. The band were led through from the backstage area, itself full of friends and fellow stars who had turned up, for this wasn't just a concert it was an Event with a capital E. Roger, John, Brian and Freddie ran through the smoke towards the noise of the crowd. The opening chords of "One Vision" came from Brian's 'fireplace' guitar and Freddie began to run closer still, drawn inexorably to the deafening roar until he was at the very edge of the stage looking down at the crowd that stretched back before him, illuminated by giant searchlights. With a cry, a snarl even, of "This is what you wanted – this is what you're gonna get", he leads the others into "Tie your Mother down" and is off on his travels, roaming the stage, climbing the giant catwalks so he can peer down from an even greater height at the crowd, who are happy to look up at him. Then he's down again, back among the other three, back to back, shoulder to shoulder with Brian May as he postures and poses. All of Knebworth's a stage, and he's the player-king, the player-Queen. The band go through their 15 years of hits. The quartet had decided at the outset when the whole tour was being planned and discussed, to include most of their greatest hits – "Bohemian Rhapsody", "Another One Bites the Dust", "Love of My Life", the whole lot. It's one of the features that gives the concert a special atmosphere – the audience seem to know the words to every song. They know the words so well that there is no problem as Freddie leads them through the scales, even though no one seems to be able to get as high up them as Freddie himself (Kiri Ke Tenawa is not among the audience).

The stage goes quiet and is strangely empty. John and Roger have gone off and there are two stools in the middle, for Brian and Freddie to sit on as they go through "Is This the World we Created", the song that summed up everyone's feelings at Live Aid a year earlier, when many heard it for the first time. There's a riveting medley of old songs – "Baby I don't care, Hello Mary Lou and Tutti Frutti", songs that were around when the band was young, around even before the four young students first got together to play. Then it's Brian May's turn, with three members of the stage crew rushing frantically after him untangling the lead from his guitar, he careers round the stage playing an intricate solo, the music in time with his running.

On the music goes; John goes off to change into shorts as Queen keep up the pace, keep up the hits. One encore is not enough; the crowd know it, Queen know it as they wait in the wings, towels around their sweating shoulders. It's two encores at least. Freddie is back in his ermine robe, all 40 pounds of sequins hanging round his shoulders, as the familiar strains of God Save the Queen ring from the crowd. A master of understatement, Freddie sings "We Are The Champions" and fully deserves to wear the crown that is perched on his head. The crowd yell hopefully for another encore, but the concert is over. But things haven't finished. As the crowd leave Knebworth, there is an exhilarating party backstage, as flamboyant as the concert. Late in the night, or late in the morning the party ends. And the tour is over.

Of course it wasn't always like this, John Deacon remembered the worst moment, and "it wasn't playing to a half empty hall somewhere or other. That was part of getting started and we expected it. It was when we were booked to play two sets and during the interval the organiser came backstage and said 'the audience don't want you back, they'd rather have the disco instead'! "But that was 15 years ago, when the four students had first got together, Queen emerging from the ruins of an earlier group, Smile. A lot of miles have been covered since then, from the tiny hall in the College of Estate Management, London – where 80 out of an invited audience of 120 turned up for the first concert – to some of the biggest rock venues in the world.

It sounds like a landmark, 15 years, as if the tour of Europe this year had some special, symbolic significance about it. To many people, inside and outside the industry, it was seen as an indication or as proof that the four stars were finally splitting up to go their separate ways. Just about the only people who took no notice of this rumour were the four stars themselves – "Sure, after all these years we have our fights", says Brian May, "but we're in a state of unstable equilibrium. We can't live with each other, and we can't live without each other". Queen saw a different logic behind the "Kind of Magic" tour. For a start, this was the year when a new album called, surprise, surprise, "A Kind of Magic" would come out. Second, the success and the euphoria generated by the Live Aid concert a year earlier had revigorated Queen with a desire to experience the energy drip-feed again. Just as fans who buy records never get to see a group if it doesn't tour, so a group doesn't get to see the fans who buy the records if it doesn't tour. Especially when you've developed, over those 15 years, a stage show that is the most stunning and spectacular in the world of rock, an extravaganza of pomp and circumstance that can't be conveyed on records. They're a band that likes and revels in the drama of a live performance, a drama that Freddie describes as "doing battle with the audience . . . I come off stage feeling as though I've been to war – and won!"

But tours, the endless travelling are tiring. "We were going to take it easy in 1986", said John Deacon, "but Live Aid was so fantastic and we got such an amazing response that it charged us up all over again".

stadium in the world, but in many ways it's the most important, the Wimbledon of rock. There aren't that many groups who can fill it once, so the knowledge that it was full for two consecutive nights was a proof and a demonstration to the four members of Queen of their power.

If it's of any interest, the architect's plans for Wembley Stadium are wrong. They are, in fact, four feet out. This may not matter much to a fan, but it nearly spelt disaster for Queen. Working to the plans, a special stage had been built, designed to fill one complete end of Wembley, and working against the clock the crew found it was precisely four feet too long. This wasn't the only problem at Wembley. The local authority are famous for their stringent regulations, and they refused permission for the gas torches that when lit flared out from the side of the stage (to make sure that Queen didn't use them on the second, and final concert, they even posted a guard on the gas cylinders all night!)

But God must be a Queen fan. On the Saturday it poured all day, drenching the 72,000 crowd and Status Quo as well. But it miraculously stopped for a while when Queen came on (not permanently, though – He doesn't like all their numbers). Freddie got wet as well as the band moved out from the covered part of the stage, to the front, as the lights were turned on the crowd. Four huge inflatable dummies of the group were released into the air. Two were hauled down by fans but two floated up to land in someone's garden miles away.

If the atmosphere at the concert was special because it was Wembley, the party afterwards was special because it was after Wembley. The group took over the Gardens night club, high over London with a huge roof garden filled with exotic food and strange sights. Members of the band joined other rock stars in impromptu jam sessions, and John Deacon didn't leave for home until 9 in the morning.

After Wembley, it was another football stadium, Maine Road, in Manchester. By now the tour was becoming a blur for the group and when they played 'Now I'm Here', they were beginning to wonder where Here was. Back to Europe, to Germany, to Vienna, on to Budapest, to France again and then Spain. The pressure was really showing by Madrid. Put four people in close physical and emotional proximity for so long and there's bound to be pressure. There was a glorious backstage fight in Madrid when nearly everything in the dressing room was destroyed. So too was a myth – everyone believes that rock stars destroy television sets in their rooms when they are angry. Well, the television set was the only thing that wasn't wrecked in Madrid. Madrid, on to Marbella – and back to England. And Knebworth. The end of the tour. A Kind of Magic had spread over Europe and it was all over.

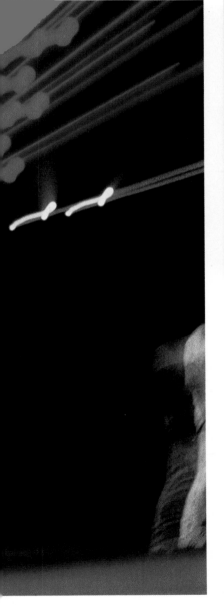

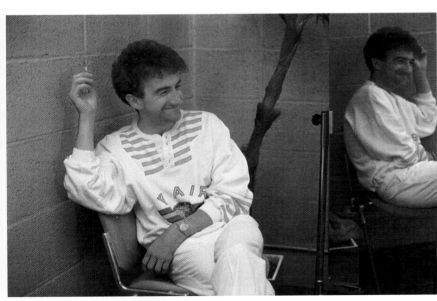

27

40

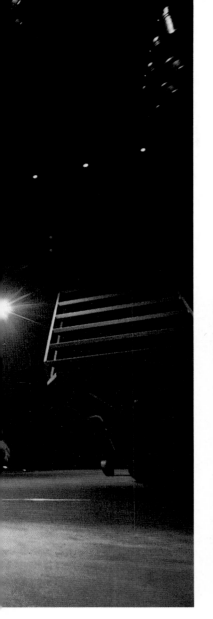

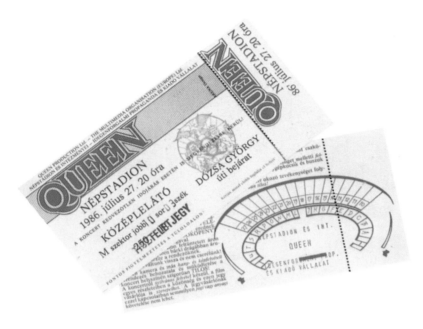

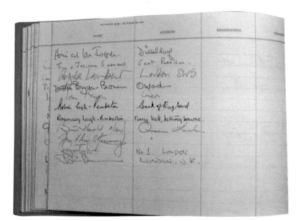

On the occasion of Queen's visit
Her Britannic Majesty's Chargé d'Affaires
and Mrs David Colvin
request the pleasure of the company of
....
at a Reception
on Thursday 24th July 1986 at seven p.m.
R.S.V.P.
182-888

Lóránffy Zsuzsanna u. 7.
Budapest II.   Please bring this card with you.

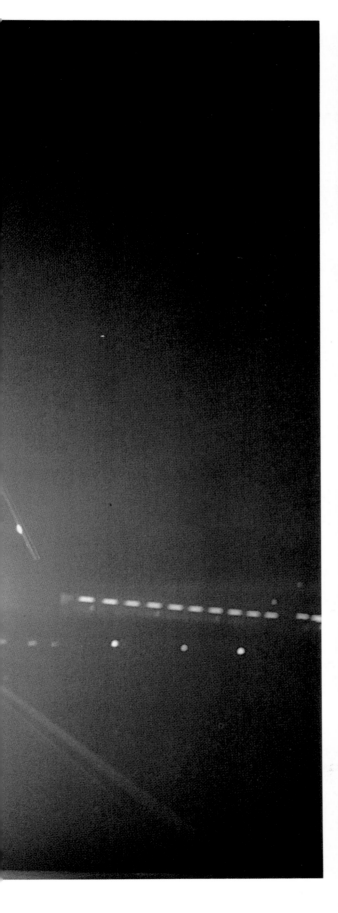

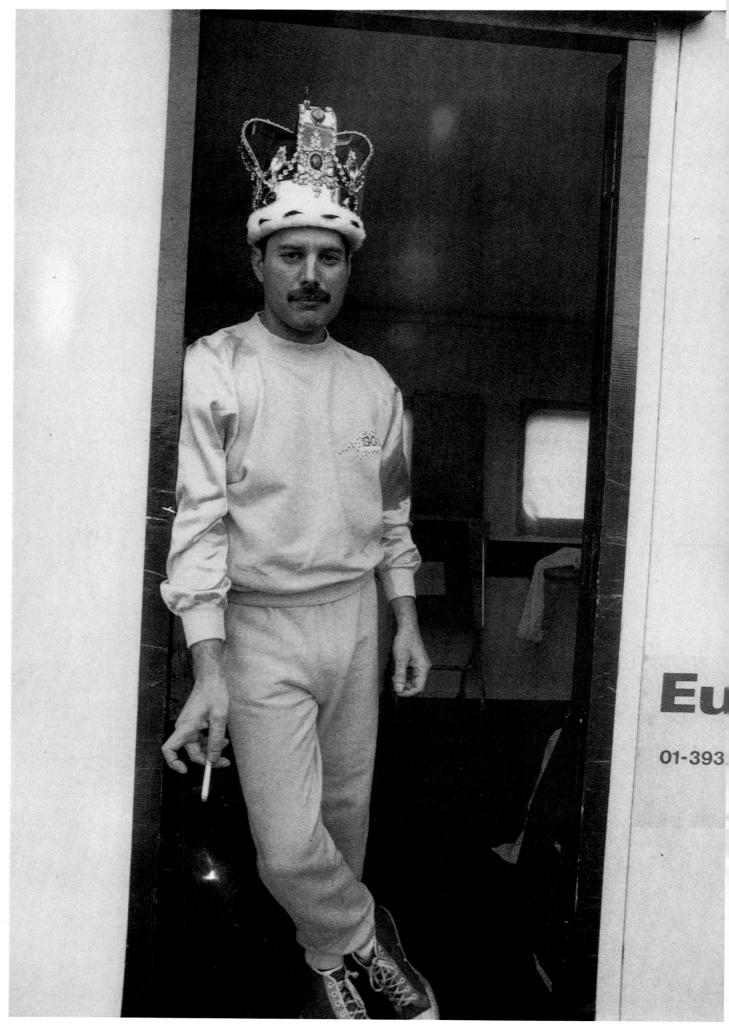

Eu

01-393

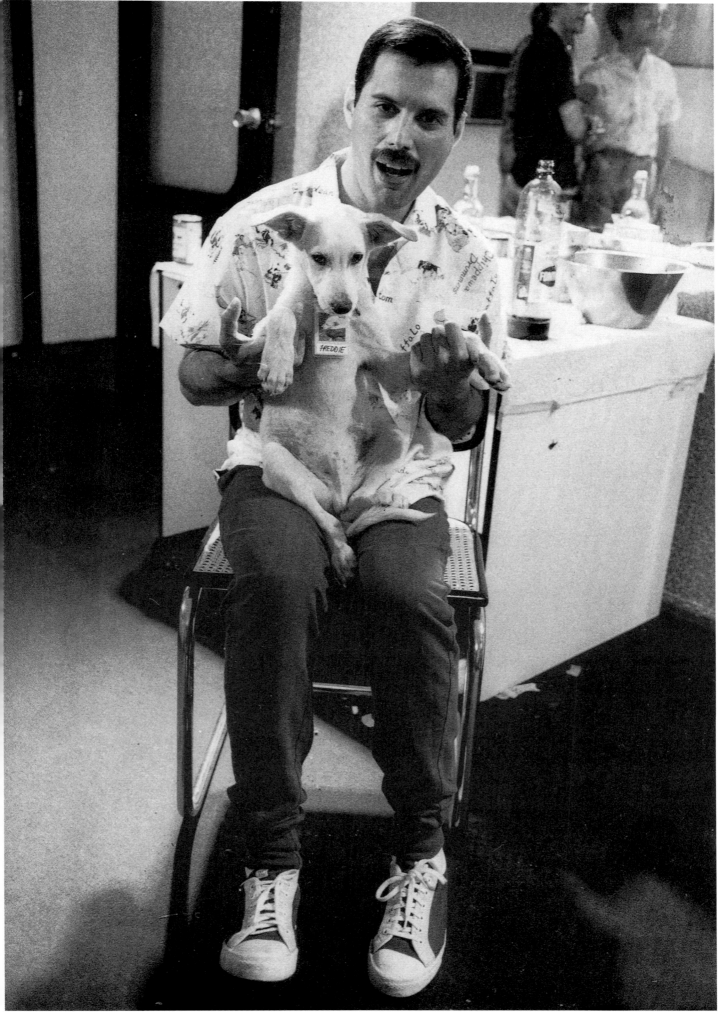

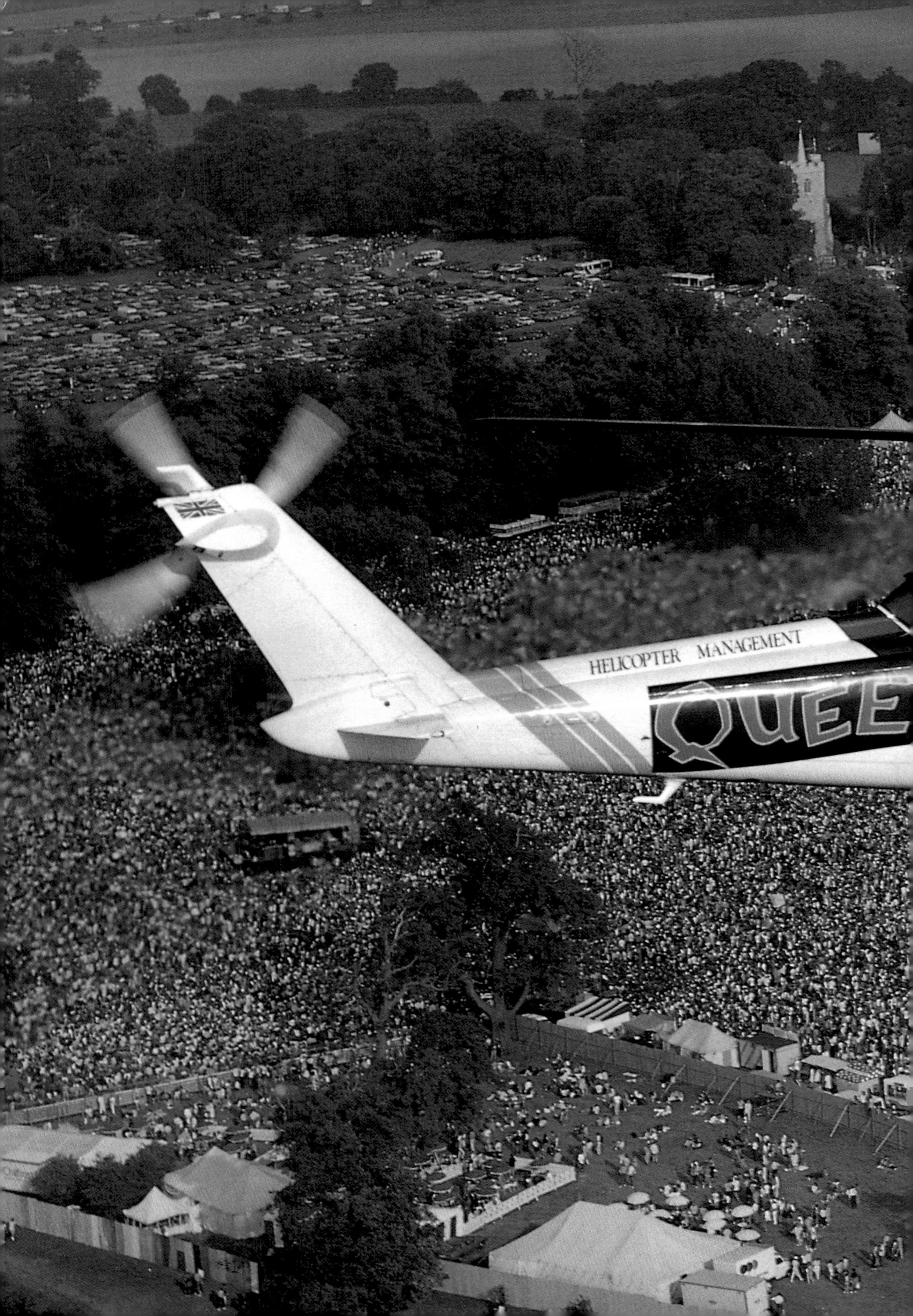
HELICOPTER MANAGEMENT
QUEE

QUEEN
SATURDAY
9th AUGUST 1986
KNEBWORTH
33679

HARVEY GOLDSMITH
PROUDLY
PRESENTS

QUEEN
Plus
Special Guests

KNEBWORTH PARK
STEVENAGE, HERTS
SATURDAY
9 AUGUST 1986

GATES OPEN 12 NOON
SHOW ENDS 10.30 p.m.

Advance tickets
£14.50 inc V.A.T.
On the Day
£16.00 inc V.A.T.

Advance tickets
£14.50 inc V.A.T.
On the Day
£16.00 inc V.A.T.

NO OVERNIGHT CAMPING
Ample Car Parking Available
Please keep the park tidy. Put your litter in
the bins provided or take it home. Thank you

KNEBWORTH PARK
SATURDAY 9th AUGUST 1986
33679

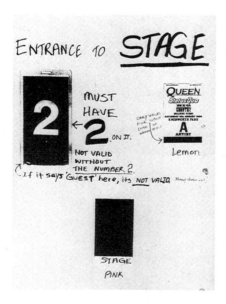

ENTRANCE TO **STAGE**

2 MUST HAVE **2** ON IT.

←

NOT VALID WITHOUT THE NUMBER 2

If it says 'GUEST' here, its NOT VALID. These than us!

QUEEN
Status Quo
etc
CHRIST
SATURDAY AUGUST 9th
KNEBWORTH PARK

ONLY VALID FOR STAGE TIME 1 of NUMBER 90 -2

A ARTIST

Lemon

STAGE
PINK

O'BRIEN'S BAR + GRILL
THE KINGS BREAKFAST
"SPOTTED DICK"
GARY MOORE
(IRISH SPECIALITY)

MARILLION À LA MODE
(FISH DISH)

QUEENS PUDDING

LEVEL 42
(SOUL FOOD)

DESERT
THE "ROYAL" BOX

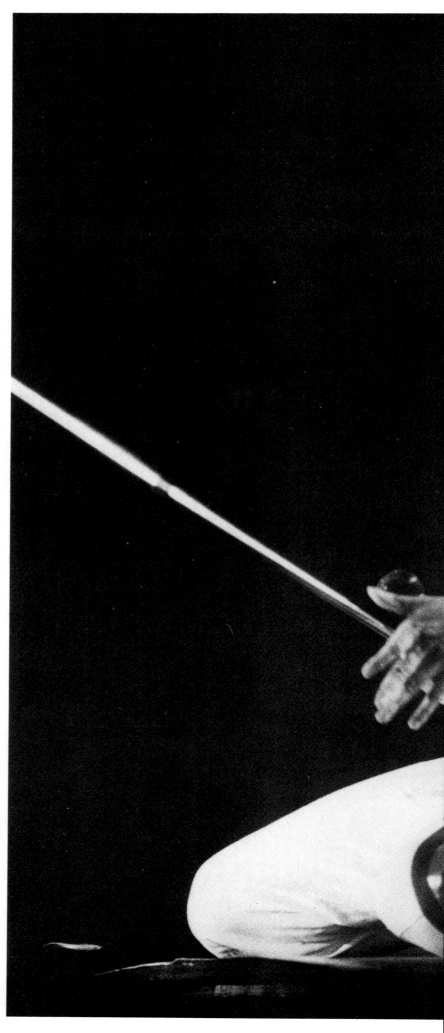

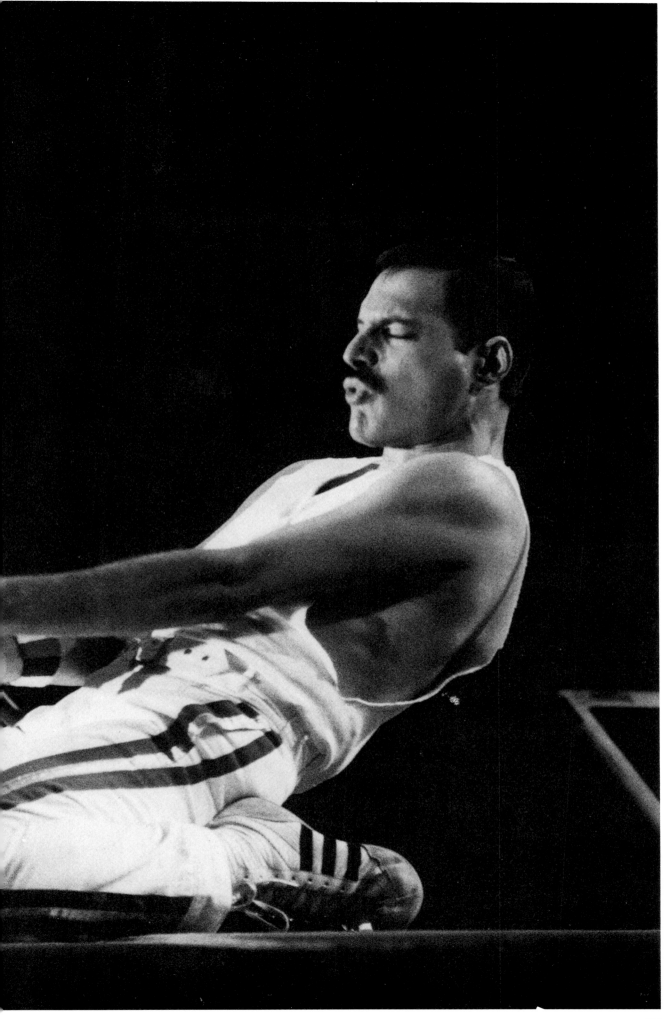

VENUE	ATTENDANCE	VENUE	ATTENDANCE
STOCKHOLM, RÅSUNDA FOTBOLL STADION	37,500	BERLIN, WALDBUEHNE	22,600
LEIDEN, GROENOOR DHAL	12,800	MUNICH, OLYMPIAHALLE	11,200
LEIDEN, GROENOOR DHAL	12,800	MUNICH, OLYMPIAHALLE	11,200
PARIS, HIPPODROME DE VINCENNES	40,000	ZURICH, HALLENSTADION	11,400
BRUSSELS, FORÊT NATIONAL	9,200	ZURICH, HALLENSTADION	11,400
LEIDEN, GROENOOR DHAL	12,800	DUBLIN, SLANE CASTLE	95,000
MANNHEIM, MAIMARKTGELÄNDE	85,700	NEWCASTLE, ST. JAMES PARK	38,000

VENUE	ATTENDANCE	VENUE	ATTENDANCE
LONDON, WEMBLEY STADIUM	72,000	FREJUS, THE AMPHITHEATRE	15,000
LONDON, WEMBLEY STADIUM	72,000	BARCELONA, MONUMENTAL PLAZA DE TOROS	18,000
MANCHESTER, MAINE ROAD	35,000	MADRID, RAYO VALLECANO	45,000
COLOGNE, MUENGERSDORFER STADION	50,000	MARBELLA, ESTADIO MUNICIPAL	37,000
VIENNA, STADTHALLE	12,000	STEVENAGE, KNEBWORTH PARK	120,000
VIENNA, STADTHALLE	12,000		
BUDAPEST, NEPSTADION	80,000		

FREDDIE MERCURY
JOHN DEACON
ROGER TAYLOR
BRIAN MAY

Additional keyboards, guitar and vocals:
Spike 'The Duke' Edney

Business management: **Jim 'Miami' Beach**
Tour production and management: **Gerry 'Uncle
Grumpy' Stickells for GLS Productions, Inc.**
Band coordinator: **Chris 'Crystal' Taylor**
Production and stage managers: **Rick 'Parnelli'
O'Brien and Mike 'M.I.' Wiesman**
Pre-production coordinator: **Brian Croft for
Samuelsons Group Plc.**
Concert sound: **James 'Trip' Khalaf for Clair
Brothers Audio U.S. & U.K.**
Monitor engineer: **Jim 'Mary' Devenney**
Sound technicians: **Rex Ray, Tom 'Midget'
Foehlinger, Barry Clair and Bill Louthe**
Lighting designer: **Roy 'Cliff' Bennett**
Lighting: **Zenith Lighting Ltd.**
Lighting director: **Simon Tutchener**
Lighting technicians: **Steve Moles, Tim Phillips,
Gerry Mott, Guy Forrester, Bob Batty, Dave Hill
for Vari-Lites and Alan Espley for Light and
Sound Design**
Guitar technician: **Brian 'Jobby' Zellis**
Keyboard and bass technicians: **Peter 'Ratty'
Hince and John 'Collie' Collins**
Drum technician: **Neil 'Moxie' Glover**
Piano tuner: **Steven Benjamins**
Rigger: **Charlie 'High Steel Drifter' Boxhall**
Carpenters: **Dave 'Batman' Irwin and Alex 'Zeus'
Alexandrou**
Band assistant: **Joe 'Liza' Fannelli**
Assistant to tour manager: **Sylvia Reed**
Wardrobe: **Tony 'Mr. Hyde' Williams**
Stage costumes: **Diana Moseley**
Physiotherapist: **Dieter 'Fizzy-O' Breit**
Security: **Wally Gore, John 'Tunbridge' Wells,
Terry Giddings, Jim Callaghan, Dave Mills and
Brendan Hyland**
Trucking: **Edwin Shirley Trucking Ltd.**
Drivers: **Mickey Conafray, Albert Sutton, Alan**

**'Vera' Moore, John 'B.J.' Lewis, George Stedman,
Ted Winfield, Nigel Auckland, Joe Harrison and
Tim Davis**
Buses: **Len Wright Travel**
Drivers: **Mick Dean and Graham Joggins**
Staging: **Edwin Shirley Staging**
Staging coordinator: **Graeme Fleming and
Henry Crallen**
Staging crew: **Tom Armstrong, Dale Scotting,
Dragon Kuzmanov and Phillip Pescod**
Set design: **Planview, Inc. John McGraw and
John Miles**
Set construction: **Kimpton Walker Ltd.**
Travel: **Trinifold Travel Ltd. Mike Hawksworth
and Alan Newing**
U.S. travel: **Air Apparent, Inc. Paula Lessel**
Accounting: **Peter Chant**
U.K. Publicity: **Roxy Meade**
U.S. Publicity: **Bryn Bridenthal**
Freight forwarders: **Rock-It Cargo Ltd and
Rock-It Cargo, Inc.**
Catering: **Toad in the Hole, Dave Keeble,
Dave Lewis, Dave Thomas, Mick 'Not Dave'
Riddle, Lindsey 'Not Dave' Beckingham and
Malcolm 'Not Dave' Barnett**
Documentary filming: **'The Torpedo Twins',
Rudi Dolezal and Hannes Rossacher**
Queen Productions Ltd: **Julie Nash, Jacky Gunn,
Christine Southard and Peter 'Feebie' Freestone**

The Official International Queen Fan Club
46 Pembridge Road, London W11 3HN, England

Queen matching printed music folios published
by IMP
A Day at the Races, A Kind of Magic, Gold,
Greatest Hits, Hot Space, Jazz, News of the
World, Queen, The Game, The Works, The
Complete Works updated.